HONEY BEAR & JAKE

+++++ A SHORT TALE +++++

By Uncle Jim
James L. Wilgus

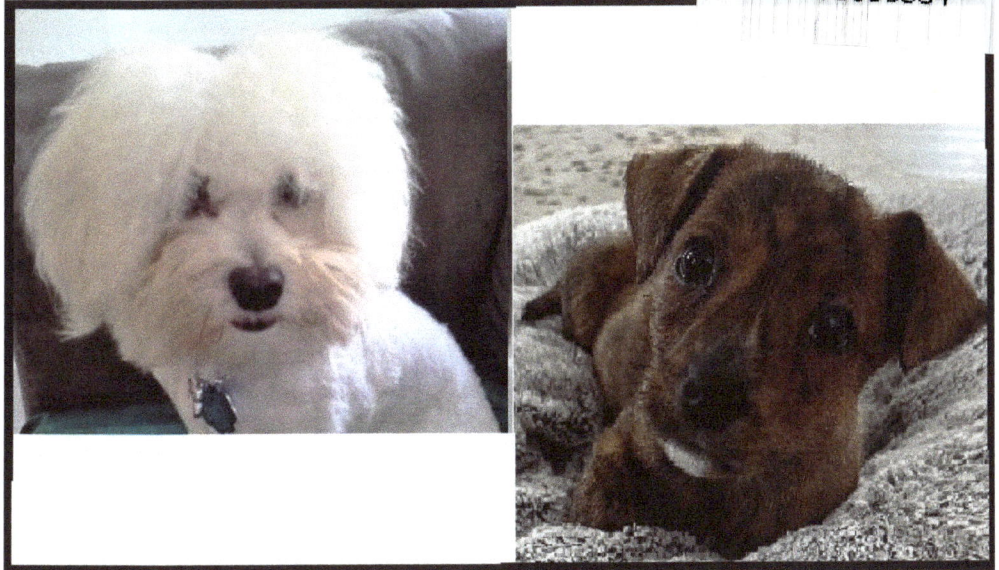

Photographs By:

Wendy Wilgus
Spencer Freedman
Audra Freedman
Bella Wilgus

This story is dedicated to our Honey Bear, a lovable and fearless puppy. We enjoyed our time together. She brought so much happiness into our home. May she rest in peace!

This is a true story which is also dedicated to all the compassionate people who rescue pets and give them a chance at life. We especially want to thank the staff and the children at the Primrose School, where Wendy teaches, for sending a beautiful card.

Published By: Wendys Marketplace, LLC
Old Bridge, NJ 08857
www.wendysmarketplace.com

Publishing Date: June 30, 2022

Printed By: Graphic Concepts Printing, Enviroprint USA
Bound Brook, New Jersey 08805

ISBN: 979-8-9871120-2-1
eISBN: 979-8-9871120-3-8

My name is Honey Bear. I'm a Maltese/Poodle, often referred to as a MultiPoo. I grew up on a large property in the woods. Wendy was my main owner and was always brushing my hair. Her mom and dad were like my valets. When Wendy was at work, they gave me treats and put me out to play. That was where I learned most everything I know. Of course, I learn something new every day as you will discover when I meet Jake.

That was the home where I learned to walk and run. I learned when it was okay to bark and when to be quiet. I learned to help dig in the garden with my valet to plant flowers. The smell of new blossoms was a pleasure we both enjoyed.

My favorite summer activity was swimming, especially on hot days. So long as my valet would stay in the water I was there. He taught me how to swim, so he believes. I think it came naturally. It didn't matter, so long as he stayed near me.

I didn't see many people while I was living in the woods, but I did see a lot of wild animals. There were deer, squirrels, raccoons, possum, turtles, frogs, groundhogs, fox, bear, rabbits, owls, wild turkeys, pheasant, vultures and a variety of flying birds. Of course there were mostly deer. They liked eating flowers, shrubs, bushes, almost anything that was growing. They even stood on their back legs to reach leaves hanging from the trees. The rabbits enjoyed eating all the green leaves from the plants and had the sweet flowers for dessert. They got up before me so I had no chance of stopping them.

My valet had put a runner line from the porch to a
large tree near the edge of the woods so I could run
back and forth. I would run forever if I didn't get
tired. I loved the outdoors and the fresh air.

Sometimes I worried my valet would forget me
outside, but I was never afraid. Every night I would be
put out before going to bed, so I was used to the dark.
I had a job to do and I did it. My job was to keep the
animals out of the yard, so they would not eat the
plants. I had to focus on the deer and rabbits. I got
lime disease so my valet put a deer fence around the
house. It kept the deer out so I just had to keep the
rabbits out.

The fence didn't keep the birds from coming into the yard. They just flew from one bird feeder to another and then back to a nearby tree. I soon learned there was no way I could jump high enough to keep them away. In truth, I really didn't want to chase them because I admired how different they were than me and all the other animals. I also noticed how different they looked from each other. They all had such beautiful colors. They seemed to get along so well taking turns at the feeders and the bird bath. They did alright for themselves without a valet.

When I saw a deer come near the fence I would run in that direction until I reached the end of my line. Then I would bark as loud as I could, but the deer just stared at me. They knew I had a set range and could not get near them. They also knew that the fence that kept them out, also kept me in. I always wondered what would happen if I had no line, or fence, and I got loose. My valets worried about that also because I was fearless. I would probably chase a deer forever.

The same was true with all the animals. I would chase them but never catch them. They always came back. Maybe this was a game we were supposed to play. To me, it was a game. I didn't mind not catching them. I was the big bad wolf in this jungle. They were like playmates even though I never got to meet them.

A New Beginning

Then one day, my family moved to a smaller house on a smaller property close to other houses. The first thing my valet did was to put up that runner line so I could run outside, but not leave the property. It wasn't as large as my old yard, but it had no hills or stairs.

No matter which house I lived in, there were always the same clouds in the sky and the same sun. At night I even saw the same moon. But the yard was different. There were squirrels and rabbits that would visit, like before, and of course, many birds. But there were no deer and other wild animals. I didn't chase the birds, I just enjoyed watching them, as before. They seemed so harmless and fragile and they never bothered me.

The runner line was something I was familiar with because that's all I knew since I was a puppy. Then one day there were men working in my yard and I was not allowed to go out to play. It happened to be a nice day so I was disappointed I had to stay in the house. Of course it was interesting to watch a bunch of strangers in my yard. I wanted to chase them away. I did my job however, looking out the glass door and yelling at them to get out of my yard. They basically ignored my bark.

By the end of the day my family let me go outside, but they didn't hook me up to the runner line. I sat on the deck for a few minutes, completely free, and slowly walked to the step onto the patio. I noticed that my family was watching me from the patio door. It felt strange not being hooked to the runner line. It was a new life in a new world.

I started running on the grass across the yard when suddenly I reached a fence. I looked around and saw the fence was completely around the entire yard. I had total freedom to run anywhere in the yard that I wanted to go. This was my new home.

I enjoyed my new freedom through the fall and into the winter. I especially loved the snow. I would use my head to snowplow a path across the deck, the patio and into the yard. Playing in the snow was my favorite winter activity since I was a puppy. My valet put a winter coat on me, but I was never cold. This was a habit since my first winter. My own fur was my coat.

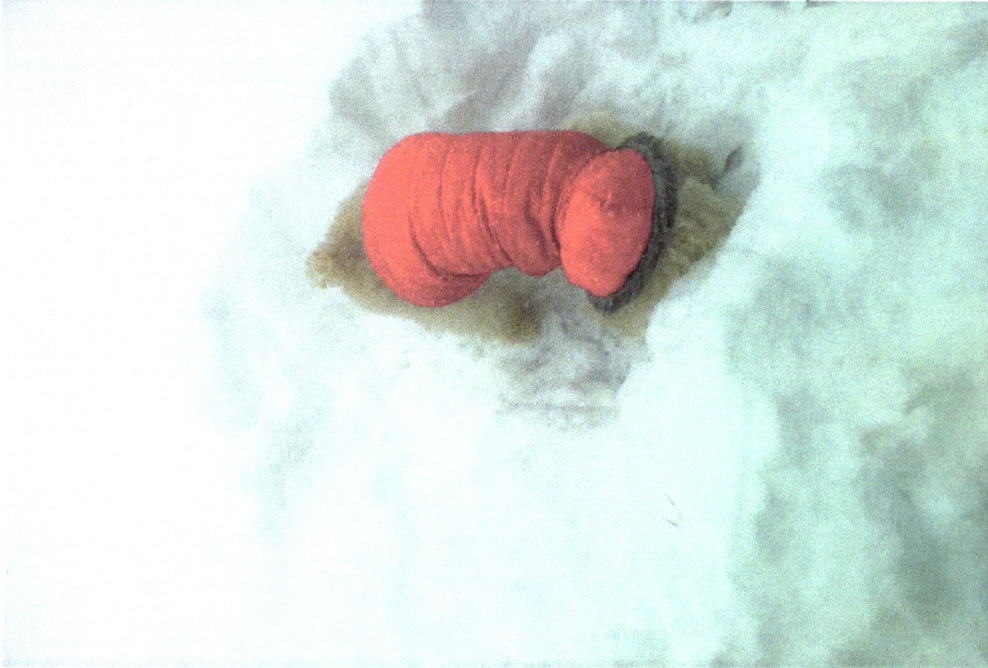

When the snow was gone, the beautiful green lawn popped up and covered the entire yard. It looked like spring was here again. I could run at full speed from one end of the yard to the other, then in circles, then explore all corners of the yard. I learned the limit of my territory but I also realized there was no limit on my freedom.

This Is Where Girl Meets Boy

One day I was watching birds in a neighbor's yard, when suddenly I saw the lady who lived there carrying a little puppy. She placed it on the ground attached it to a leash. The puppy just sat there. I walked up to the fence to get a closer look. The lady backed away from the puppy and said "Jake, come!" She tugged on the leash so the little guy walked toward her. I liked his name. It was a boy dog. It looked like he had a valet also. This was so exciting.

It seemed I had a new friend. He was brown with short hair, the opposite of my white long hair. We looked nothing like each other, but I knew we were both dogs. We were neighbors. I thought we should get along with each other.

I shouted out, "Hi Jake, my name's Honey Bear." He didn't respond, but I know he heard me because he scratched the valet's leg as he was looking at me. It was a signal to pick him up, so his valet did and took him back into the house.

Jake was a puppy, probably a few months old. He came from a kennel in another state where he was abandoned and was about to be put to sleep, forever. The neighbors decided to rescue him and give him a home where he could grow up with a loving family. That was Jake's lucky day.

A few days went by and I saw my valet working with Jake's other valet putting up a runner line like I had. They gave Jake the freedom to run across the yard without the valet's holding a leash running behind. This was freedom for all.

At first Jake wasn't sure what to do when he was hooked up to the line. His valet walked back to the house, looking over his shoulder as he and Jake stared at each other. The valet sat on his deck to see what Jake would do, as if he was waiting to be entertained by some circus animal.

I called to Jake and invited him to come by the fence so we could get to know each other. Jake was smaller than me, and when the grass wasn't cut I could hardly see him. He finally came over to visit and we smelled each other for a long time. I think he was trying to steal a kiss.

He wasn't very talkative because he was still getting used to his new home and new family. I can understand being shy. I've been there.

He liked jumping up and down. Maybe he jumped so he could see better over the high grass, or maybe he was just excited to see me. To make him feel at home, I would jump along with him.

When the grass was cut, I could see Jake better and he was able to run faster. He would run along his side of the fence and I would run along on my side keeping pace with him. This was a fun part of my day. He was still not sure where the line ended so he always made sudden stops. That was funny to watch, but when I first did it 10 years ago, I didn't find it so funny.

I know he will learn his limits very soon. He will overcome being shy and will get along with all the other animals, just as he and I will get to be the best of friends. Someday he will be bigger than me and probably run much faster. Until then, I am going to enjoy my new friend Jake.

++++++++++++++++++++++++++++++++
Almost The End
++++++++++++++++++++++++++++++++

A note from the author: This is where this story was supposed to end, unless their relationship would inspire me to write a follow up story. But the sequel in the affairs of Honey Bear and Jake was not meant to be, yet, I cannot let this story end without a final word from Honey Bear.

The Beginning Of The End

Jake was a fireball, full of energy. He was my first and only boyfriend. About a month went by and I realized that while Jake was growing, my health was getting worse. Somedays I would just sit on my deck waiting for Jake to come out. I could only watch him run and jump around the yard as if to amuse me. I was entertained, but sad that I was not able to join him.

My failing health became alarming to my valets. I did not want to eat, and when I drank water it just made me throw up. It was Memorial Day and my doctor was not working, so my valets took me to an animal hospital. The doctor gave me fluids, because my body was dry, and medicine to stop me from throwing up. My valet let me sleep wherever I wanted to that night. I just plopped on the living room floor next to my lifetime buddy, Socks. He knew I was sick and wanted to watch over me throughout the night. Socks was there when I first came home 10 years ago. He protected me when I was a baby and now Socks is here again to look over me in my final days.

The next morning I was worse. I had no appetite and could not drink. My valet would squirt water in my mouth but it would not stay down. The next day my vet was available so we went to see him. He took my blood, tested me for diabetes, and gave me medicine for a stomach infection. The doctor was shocked to see my blood sugar was 5 times normal for a puppy so he gave me insulin for diabetes. The doctor said he would call the next day with the blood test results, but I should come back this evening for another insulin shot.

After another day the doctor called and asked us to visit him anytime that day. My valets picked me up and we drove to my vet. He said in addition to serious diabetes, there is the more serious problem of a failing kidney. He explained that with a failing kidney I would need periodic dialysis treatments. For humans this is often done until a kidney donor can be found. With animals doctors do not transplant kidneys. His recommendation was to put me to sleep forever.

My valets told the doctor that before that decision is made they want to bring me home for my rightful owner to hug me one more time before making that decision. Wendy is my official owner and she was working during the day. My valets kept trading places as to who would hold me while we waited for Wendy to come home.

The news did not go well with Wendy and she insisted that I be allowed to pass away on my own terms. She got her wish and I survived the night. The next morning was no better than the last 5 days. Wendy gave me a big hug and a kiss, like every morning, and went off to work.

My valets tried squirting water and a high protein drink in my mouth but I kept spitting it up. As my valet was holding me, I heard him tell his wife that I would stop breathing for almost a minute, then suddenly take a deep breath. This went on all morning as I tried looking out the window for Jake, but my vision was too blurry to focus. "I think we are losing her, but I still feel a heartbeat" said my valet. Suddenly I stopped breathing completely. I could no longer see, or hear anything, or feel the comfort of my valet's arms.

I had no more pain. There was nothing more anyone could have done. The last thing I remember was my valet's tears on my fur. Wendy got her wish, I passed away on my own terms. Then I saw the clouds passing by as I entered Puppy Heaven. I think I'll be watching below now to see how Jake grows up.

+++++++++++++++++++++++++++++++
That Is The End Of Honey Bear's Story
+++++++++++++++++++++++++++++++

WITH SYMPATHY
In the Loss of Honey Bear

They will not go quietly,
the pets who've shared our lives.
In subtle ways they let us know
their spirit still survives.
Old habits still can make us
think we hear them at the door
Or step back when we drop
a tasty morsel on the floor.

YUMMY

A New Beginning

It isn't right for a story to end on a sad note, so I am pleased to say this story has a happy ending. After 2 days with an emptiness in her heart, Wendy adopted a new puppy, a SilkyPoo, and named it CUPCAKE. So a new story begins.

www.ingramcontent.com/pod-product-compliance
Lightning Source LLC
Chambersburg PA
CBHW052126030426

42335CB00025B/3131